ENDORSEMENTS

Kenny Vaughan's book paints for us a master-piece of hope for those in the midst of difficult circumstances. His "wild ride up the ramp of life" is one with which we can all immediately identify. He shows us how to recognize God's sovereign hand in all of life, reminding us that the Lord uses both good and not so good to mold and shape us for His glory and His pur-poses. Those who read this book will learn both how to view trials and struggles and how to claim the joy of God's presence and direction in them. One of the great assets of the book is that Kenny backs up everything with the power and instruction of God's Word.

Martin Dittmar
Athletic Chaplain
Purdue University

Do you need a rudder on your ship? *Trials to Trophies* is an amazing story of how God changed one man's life and how his now rock-solid faith is spreading like an epidemic to those who need it most. It has already strengthened the faith of thousands of young people, adults, athletes, military personnel, public servants, and professionals. In a society reliant on anti-depressants, this book should be prescribed.

Andrew Wilson
President/founder
Lone Star Lifting

Trials to Trophies is a must-read for anyone being held back in life by fear and the frustration that comes from not reaching their full potential. This book has long been anticipated by those familiar with Kenny's own story of a lifelong battle with fear and his ultimate victory over the debilitating condition.

You'll laugh, you'll cry, you'll cheer, and when you're finished reading you'll claim your victory too. Do yourself and those you love a favor—buy this book, read this book. It might just change your life.

Jeff Knight
Minister/co-founder
International Currency

Kenny Vaughan is a fierce competitor with a warrior's instinct. His remarkable victory over years of doubt and fear and his unshakable faith in God inspired the soldiers within my battalion as we prepared to deploy to Afghanistan for Operation Enduring Freedom and to Iraq for Operation Iraqi Freedom. Most of these soldiers wore a Shield of Strength as a personal reminder that God was with them wherever they went.

David E. Dodd
Lieutenant Colonel
United States Army

Trials.
to
Trophies

Trials to Trophies

THE POWER OF FAITH IN ADVERSITY

JOHN KENNEDY VAUGHAN

BROWN BOOKS PUBLISHING GROUP
DALLAS, TEXAS

TRIALS TO TROPHIES:
THE POWER OF FAITH IN ADVERSITY

For information, please contact
Brown Books Publishing Group
16200 North Dallas Parkway,
Suite 170, Dallas, Texas 75248
www.brownbooks.com
972-381-0009

ISBN 0-9753907-0-8
LCCN 2004116009
First printing, January 2005; second printing, October 2005

Note to Readers

I have learned that—though hard work and discipline are important—these have little to do with overcoming fear. Acting on God's word, no matter our circumstances, feelings, or emotions is the only thing I have found that will move us from fear to supernatural boldness, and allow us to function with a sound mind through any trial.

It's not how straight the path or how many roadblocks and detours along the route, how smooth or rocky the way, but what we learn on the journey that matters, how much closer to God we finish, and how we use what He has taught us on the way.

—John Kennedy Vaughan

Love the Lord your
God with all your heart
and all your soul and with
all your mind. . . . Love
your neighbor as yourself.
Matthew 22:37-39

DEDICATION

This story is for every athlete, soldier, and student; every spouse, parent, and single parent; every businessman and woman; every son and daughter—every soul who desperately needs to see that God is much bigger and more powerful than their own struggles, fears, and emotions.

Special thanks to the soldier of the 86th Signal Battalion, wherever you are right now, who asked that I write this story down. This book began as my letter to you. So it is fitting that I dedicate it to you and end it with a personal message to you in the epilogue. I extend my thanks to you for the sacrifices you and your family members make every day for me and for my family. I lift up a special prayer every day for your safety and for provisions for your family. And I pray that you will have the opportunity to read this message and that you and others will come to know and remember that "[You] can do all things through Christ who strengthens [you]." Philippians 4: 13.

I believe that two commandments in Matthew 22:37–39 give the basics for turning from fear to a life of victory:

Love the Lord your God with all your heart and all your soul and with all your mind.

—God's first and greatest commandment; and

Love your neighbor as yourself.

I have asked God many times what I must do to keep my blessings, since I have never been sure what I did to receive them in the first place. Every time He has impressed on my heart to obey the greatest commandment to love Him.

I have learned that the more God blesses me, the more closely others will look at my life, and therefore the greater my responsibility to love others as myself.

God wants us to love Him with all our hearts, so He can work in our lives and guide us. He wants us to love our neighbor as we love ourselves, so He can bless us for the benefit of His Kingdom. If we do not love Him, we will not allow Him to guide us. We will stumble over the blessings He has given us, and we will fall. If we do not love our neighbor, we are likely to wage the blessings we receive against our neighbor in some way, causing our neighbor to stumble or fall.

Now, let me tell you my story. It is the story of how God became more real and alive to me when I was the weakest, and when my own capabilities were stretched to the maximum and fell short, except for Him.

You will have to look back with me a couple of decades, but the story is timeless, and new chapters are opening every day as God takes the struggles in my past and gives them meaning today and into the future, beyond what you and I can ever know. He will do the same for you if you will let Him.

If there is a hero in this story, it is most certainly God. He took me from trial to trophy in a way that has changed my life and spilled over in a calling to share with others, that their lives might be changed too.

I will be strong and courageous. I will not be terrified, or discouraged; for the Lord my God is with me wherever I go.

Joshua 1:9

TABLE OF CONTENTS

ACKNOWLEDGMENTS xvii

PREFACE xxi

INTRODUCTION xxix

PROLOGUE xxxiii

PART ONE
  LEARNING THE ROPES 1

    CHAPTER ONE
      PRODIGAL STUDENT 2

    CHAPTER TWO
      HUMBLE BEGINNINGS 5

PART TWO
  THE TRIALS 9

    CHAPTER THREE
      THE COMPETITION 10

    CHAPTER FOUR
      SUCCESS NOSEDIVES 14

    CHAPTER FIVE
      LETTING GO OF FAITH 17

    CHAPTER SIX
      TIME OUT 21

    CHAPTER SEVEN
      TIME IN 24

CHAPTER EIGHT
GIVING IT UP 33

CHAPTER NINE
TAKING IT BACK 35

CHAPTER TEN
PERSEVERING 40

CHAPTER ELEVEN
NO FEAR 45

CHAPTER TWELVE
THE STARTING DOCK 49

CHAPTER THIRTEEN
NO WAY TO LOSE 53

CHAPTER FOURTEEN
NO WAY TO WIN 57

PART THREE
THE TROPHY **63**

CHAPTER FIFTEEN
THE VICTORY 64

CHAPTER SIXTEEN
IN VICTORY'S WAKE 68

CHAPTER SEVENTEEN
SHIELDS OF STRENGTH 74

CHAPTER EIGHTEEN
FROM TRIALS TO TROPHIES 93

EPILOGUE **98**

LETTER TO THE SOLDIER OF THE 86TH BATTALION **103**

ACKNOWLEDGMENTS

I want to thank my parents Robert and Alice Vaughan for the countless hours they spent pulling us skiing every day of the summer, for all the personal sacrifices they made because they always put us first, for the love and discipline we constantly received, for teaching us good work ethics, and for pouring all the wisdom they could into us.

I want to thank my wife, Tammie, for leading me to the Lord. Tammie supported me and believed in me when I needed it most. Her love and stability are the foundation to my testimony and, next to the Lord, she is my greatest source of strength.

I want to thank Tammie's parents, Frank and Eloise Roccaforte, for taking me as their own, and for raising Tammie to love the Lord and others with such a sincere heart.

I want to thank my sister Bonnie and my brother Gabe for picking me up the many times I fell and for challenging me to be a better person and athlete. The three of us have always been very close and each other's greatest fans.

I want to thank my Pastor and Uncle Richard Vaughan and David Hinson for being my spiritual mentors.

I want to thank my ski coach and boat driver Charlie Fontenot for believing in me when I did not believe in myself and for the years he's spent teaching and encouraging me to be a champion.

I want to thank Command Sergeant Major Jacqui Clay, Chaplain Larry Toney, Mr. and Mrs. Jim Blanchard, and Chaplain Gregory Schannep for taking the first Shields of Strength to the military.

I want to thank Lt. Col. David Dodd, his wife Sharon, and their daughters, Caitlin and Grace, for their service to our country, for sharing the shields with so many members of the military, and for the Dodd family's wonderful friendship.

I want to thank Lt. Col. Dean Trieble and his wife D. J. Trieble for helping to reach over 30,000 US Marines in Iraq and around the world with a reminder of God's word, for their friendship and their service to our nation.

I want to thank Russell Rippetoe for giving his life in defense of our country, and his parents Lt. Col. Joe Rippetoe and Mrs. Rippetoe for their continued support of Shields of Strength. The Rippetoe family has paid the ultimate price yet remain the ultimate patriots.

I would like to thank Mark Alexander and *The Federalist* readers for helping to fund over 50,000 Shields of Strength for US Marines, sailors, and soldiers in Iraq.

I want to thank Marcia Davis for taking a letter I wrote to a soldier, pouring her heart into it and helping me transform it into *Trials to Trophies.*

I can do all things
through Christ who
strengthens me.

Phil. 4:13

PREFACE

John Kennedy Vaughan's father named John after the late John F. Kennedy, Jr.—from the memory of the image of that little boy saluting his famous father's flag-covered coffin as the funeral procession made its way toward Arlington National Cemetery. The small boy's relentless courage and honor in the face of overwhelming adversity was something John Kennedy Vaughan's father wanted to pass on to his son. And many say that, indeed, John Kennedy (Kenny) Vaughan's life has been marked with that very same courage and honor.

Kenny Vaughan lives his life driven by a stubborn faith, a quest for excellence he pursues with uncompromising determination, a gentle spirit sensitive to others, and a heart wide open to God. Vaughan steps up to personal and professional challenges with confidence based on careful reasoning, considerable prayer, and mighty faith in a powerful God. His life is a mirror of his faith and fortitude.

After he learned to ski at age eleven, his heart was set on becoming a champion water-skier. After he met and married his wife Tammie, his heart was set on being the best husband he could be, and after their daughters Faith and Grace were born, his purpose broadened to include being the best dad to them he could be. When he started his own business, the same quest for excellence prevailed over his entrepreneurial pursuits.

As a champion athlete commissioned to share his faith, Kenny Vaughan's mission has stretched from the organization he founded in 1998—Athletes for Christ—to the four corners of the globe. He made his first Shields of Strength Scripture-inscribed dog tag necklaces in 1997, never realizing the impact the necklaces would have in the years to come or the number of people who would be comforted and encouraged by wearing these special tags.

His first necklaces were personal keepsakes to help him remember all that God had shown him about living in faith and overcoming fear, as he competed in the US Nationals ski jump competition. As friends, associates, and even total strangers saw the dog tag necklaces and asked Vaughan about them, he would take them off and give them away. Soon, he found himself giving so many away, and getting so many requests for them, that it was more economical to find a way to produce the necklaces instead of ordering replacements for himself.

When US troops were first deployed to Afghanistan, shortly after the terrorist attacks of September 11, 2001, Command Sergeant Major Jacqui Clay requested Shields of Strength for the troops in her charge. It wasn't long before US soldiers of every rank and in every military branch began wearing the necklaces alongside their military-issued dog tags. Military families began wearing the shields as a spiritual covering for their family members in military service or in memory or honor of lost loved ones who had made the ultimate sacrifice in the fight for freedom in Afghanistan and Iraq.

In February of 2003, Vaughan was fishing on an East Texas lake when the Columbia Space Shuttle blew apart. He remembers the noise as the shuttle exploded and debris shot across several states. That day as he fished, he thought about the crew and their families, and decided to make a special NASA shield, honoring the lost astronauts, and as a reminder for the men and women of NASA to be strong and courageous—not terrified or discouraged—for the Lord their God is with them wherever they go. Vaughan presented NASA with the custom shields in November 2003.

In December 2003, Vaughan was invited by his good friend Lt. Col. David Dodd to share his story at a Pentagon Prayer Breakfast for military officers. After his talk, Vaughan was able to personally greet each officer and hand each one a Shield of Strength. At the Pentagon, he met several high-ranking government officials who wore the Shields of Strength and said their family members wore them as well. He was greeted by Acting Secretary of the Army and retired Col. Les Brownlee. Dodd presented Vaughan with a flag, encased, with the inscription that reads: "This flag was flown in Baghdad, Iraq, in honor of Mr. Kenny Vaughan. America's soldiers salute you for sharing God's word and for providing Shields of Strength to empower them during Operation Enduring Freedom and Operation Iraqi Freedom."

During his Washington trip, Vaughan was joined by retired Lt. Col. Joe Rippetoe, who was the father of Capt. Russell B. Rippetoe, the first American soldier of Operation Iraqi Freedom to be buried in Arlington National Cemetery. When Capt. Rippetoe was killed, he was wearing his Shield of Strength dog tag alongside his military-issued tag. Both Dodd and Rippetoe accompanied Vaughan to the Pentagon breakfast and later to visit Arlington Memorial Cemetery, where a burial service was underway, honoring another fallen soldier. That day Vaughan and Dodd looked in on several injured soldiers at Walter Reed Hospital. Of that trip, Vaughan said, "In a year I usually realize a few defining moments, but this one day, which I will never forget, was an epiphany—truly one of the most memorable times I have known."

In 2004, Vaughan made his millionth shield. By then, the necklaces were being worn by hundreds of thousands of US military men and women serving in the Middle East and across the globe and by journalists covering the war and post-war conflicts in Iraq. Today, war veterans, athletes, youth, and adults in all seasons, stages of faith, and walks of life find confidence and comfort in wearing the shields and encouragement in the shields' Scriptures.

The story told in this book conveys more about Kenny than he allows in this passage. Kenny Vaughan has been described as humble to a fault. He leads without show, giving his best and striving to achieve with an intense purpose, with neither pride nor pretense. Kenny seems to bring forth the best in others. He's quick to say his successes reflect God's glory.

Those who've met Kenny notice the steady gaze of sea-blue eyes, the quick flash of his friendly smile, a firm handshake, and a kind and caring countenance that puts one instantly at ease. The disciplined training of an elite athlete is evident in his build and carriage, and a Texas accent slides across his soft-spoken conversation. He is polite, sincere, engaging, and encouraging.

It's obvious that Kenny Vaughan has an unquenchable desire to be used by God. His willingness spills over to challenge and give courage to others.

In the pages of this book, Kenny Vaughan shares his story. He tells it, not so you will think well of him, but so you may be encouraged, come closer to God, be called to step out in limitless faith to reach beyond your dreams, and serve the Lord daily without fear or hesitation.

Kenny Vaughan lives with his wife and daughters in Beaumont, Texas. A USA National water ski jump champion, he continues to compete. Vaughan has been interviewed by a host of national print and broadcast media and has been invited to share his story at athletic, military, and Christian gatherings across the country.

(Compiled by freelance writer Marcia Davis from interviews with Kenny Vaughan, his friends, and his family.)

If my people, who are called by my name, will humble themselves and pray . . . I will hear from heaven and will forgive their sins and will heal their land.

AFC

2 Chronicles 7:14

Shields of Strength

INTRODUCTION

A weary US soldier skittishly standing watch in the midnight hours at a security checkpoint in the Middle East; a frightened young woman being rushed through the doors of the hospital delivery room; a seventy-five-year-old widow diagnosed with brain cancer and struggling to take a step; a businessman on the brink of bankruptcy; a freckle-faced teen dreading a mid-morning math exam and basketball tryouts after school—what could they possibly have in common?

Visible on each is the silver glint of a small and thin, inscribed, oblong drop—a dog tag necklace—a Shield of Strength. Invisible on each is the point of turning from fear to faith, from gut-led to guided by the God of grace, from merely surviving to living a life of victory.

After water ski jumper Kenny Vaughan discovered that his biggest challenge in ski competition was conquering his fear, not in jumping farther than his competition, he bought some dog tag necklaces and had them engraved with the Scriptures, which had helped him wage his faith over fear.

The shields were his way to remember the moment he made a critical choice to live in faith and not fear, a decision he made while skimming across the water at top speed, approaching the ski ramp, making the deciding jump for the national championship. That decision changed his course from a heartbreaking pattern of difficult defeats to a promising future. When there was no way to win, he found victory in gaining a deeper faith in God and greater insight as to how God can turn hopeless trials into timeless trophies that brighten our lives and the lives of others.

He began sending the dog tag necklaces to friends and associates as tokens of courage, faith, and focus in the face of challenge. He would pull his necklace off and give it to anyone who asked about getting one like it. Soon, requests for the necklaces began pouring in from everywhere.

When several Christian bookstore chains started stocking the necklaces, the tags quickly caught on with members of every generation.

Soon, military chaplains began requesting the necklaces for the troops under their charge. By the summer of 2003, more than 100,000 Shields of Strength had been sent to soldiers serving in military bases in the United States and overseas. Another 500,000 were being worn by civilians across the country. Now, requests for more of the necklaces come in every day from all over the world. Entire battalions serving in the Middle East and in Afghanistan are wearing the shields.

Lives across the country are being saved and changed through the Scriptures and salvation prayer inscribed on the tags.

Trials to Trophies is a story about Shields of Strength and a battle between fear and faith. In this true life adventure with God, top skier Kenny Vaughan—founder of Athletes for Christ—shares truths he learned about life's challenges and the stubborn faith that turned his trial into a trophy.

Everything in my life is marked as before or after that moment in 1996. It was the USA Water Ski National Championship competition in Fort Walton Beach, Florida. I was skimming across the water; my speed behind the boat was approaching sixty miles an hour. The long distance jump would take me approximately three stories high in the sky for a distance of about three quarters of the length of a football field.

For seventeen years, I had been working toward this day with rigorous physical training and discipline, and by pushing and perfecting my skills. I would never be more ready physically.

That day I learned that one cannot win a spiritual battle with only physical training. And I learned that faith in God is not something you can halfway, almost, or sometimes have. He will bring you to a day when you either have faith in Him or you don't. He will challenge you out of cautious faith to absolute faith. That's what He did to me.

At nationals that year, sixty of the country's best skiers were competing for the title. The skier before me had jumped five feet further than my personal best. My mind was waterlogged with worry and the boat pulling me seemed weighed down with my doubt. On my second of three jumps, I had hung my right ski on the side of the ramp, snapping off the rudder and tearing the ski boot that held my foot to the ski. Between my second and last jump, I had time to change the rudder, but no time to fix the boot.

The judges called time for me, and I knew I must ski then or forfeit. There was really no way for me to win with a torn ski boot, but the boat accelerated and I was up. The water was smooth, but the choppy waves of my emotions swirled around me, threatening to throw me off balance. My inner turmoil swelled, fed by years of almost winning, years of getting close but never quite making the mark of a champion, of living the trial but never going home with the trophy. Moments in time of believing in the power of God, but never fully testing that faith, had led to years of grabbing on to the ski rope more tightly than I held on to God. Before that time, my fear had always propelled me toward failure at a greater speed than any boat could have pulled me.

Heading for the ramp, the wake of emotion broke with enough force to suck me under. I knew I was nearing the ramp with a speed too slow and a position too narrow on the boat. I could feel a part of me watching from the dock, then turning slowly and slinking away in defeat. All I could possibly do was lose, again . . .

I caught a glimpse of the words my girlfriend had painted on the handle of my tow rope, a

Scripture from Philippians 4:13: "I can do all things through Christ who strengthens me." I decided that this time I wouldn't let my fear finish for me. I would finish to the glory of God and let Him take me all the way to victory or defeat. This time I would live out my faith to my last ounce of strength and concentration.

In retrospect, I see how God brought me to that moment. Every day since that moment, He shows me more about why He took me through the trials the way He did. Every day, I find more meaning in my wild ride up the ramp, holding so tightly to His hand.

But perhaps I should go back and start at the beginning . . . on that hot June day, so many trials ago, when my parents decided to teach us—my brother and sister and me—to water-ski.

For I am confident of this very thing, that He who began a good work in you will perfect it until the day of Christ Jesus.

Philippians 1:6

PART ONE

LEARNING THE ROPES

CHAPTER ONE

PRODIGAL STUDENT

"Call to Me, and I will answer you, and show you great and mighty things, which you do not know."

Jeremiah 33:3

"Many are the plans in a man's heart, but it is the Lord's purpose that prevails."

Proverbs: 19:21

I grew up around the water, fishing and boating.

I was ten when my uncle invited my family to his lake house for the 4th of July holiday weekend.

My parents decided to teach us—my brother and sister and me—to ski before the holiday.

My first ski equipment may have been crude, but the rough rope and broken broomstick we used as a ski tow handle must have tied a rope around my heart and bound me with a love for the sport that has never grown slack. The boat, a fourteen-foot flat bottom boat with a fifteen-horsepower Evinrude motor, pulled us on a sheet of plywood my dad had cut into a three-foot circle.

The plywood was easy to "ski" on, and my sister, brother, and I could all ride on it at the same time. My mother and father spent hours pulling us behind the boat, up and down the river on the plywood disk.

The week before we left for my uncle's lake house, my parents bought us a $35 pair of water skis. Those water skis turned the good time I was having into a comedy of errors for me. I had trouble getting up on the real skis, and when I did manage to pull myself up on them, I had no control and fell. It only took a couple of tries before I was waterlogged and disenchanted with the whole idea. I went back to fishing.

But before long, I heard the hum of the boat nearby and looked up to see my sister skiing down the river. I dropped my rod and ran to the water's edge, waving frantically and yelling at my dad to bring the boat back for me so I could try again.

Since I did not want to let my younger sister accomplish something that I couldn't do, my motivation to ski was stronger the second time around. I willed myself to stay up and gain control, and before long I found my ski legs, preserved my pride, and was gliding down the river behind the Evinrude.

I could never imagine all that was to follow this little sibling rivalry and my small taste of victory.

The Kingdom of heaven is like a mustard seed planted in a field. It is the smallest of all seeds, but it becomes the largest of all trees.

Matthew 13:31-32

Shields of Strength

CHAPTER TWO

HUMBLE BEGINNINGS

"Do not despise small beginnings and don't do anything halfway—because you can't imagine all that God may be planning to build on your actions."
—*John Kennedy Vaughan*

Today I ski on the most advanced skis in the world and behind the world's most powerful competition ski boats. I wear as many as twelve pieces of equipment for safety and performance enhancement, and any one of those pieces costs more than my father paid for all of the equipment I used while learning to ski.

My first ski equipment was makeshift and crude, but crafted out of love by my father.

Beginnings do not have to be fancy to be meaningful. I have learned not to discount the humble and the simple beginnings in life.

God can take little and make much. And aren't we glad! The Bible is filled with such accounts. In Matthew 13:31, Jesus says: "The kingdom of heaven is like a mustard seed, which a man took and planted in his field. Though it is the smallest of all seeds, when it grows, it is the largest of garden plants and becomes a tree, so that the birds of the air come and perch in its branches."

In Matthew, chapter 25, Jesus tells a story of three men who were given talents, each according to his ability. The more ability, the more talents the master gave them. Two of the men took the several talents they were given and multiplied them. To these men, their master said, "Well done, my good and faithful servants. You have been faithful with a few things; I will put you in charge of many things." The third servant took the only talent he had been given and buried it. He had the least to lose and the biggest fear of all the men. To him, the master said, "You wicked, lazy servant." The master took the talent from him, gave it to the one who worked the hardest to multiply his talents, and said, "For everyone who has will be given more, and he will have an abundance. Whoever does not have, even what he has will be taken away from him."

What I have learned and what I believe God is trying to say with both of these stories is that He wants us to take what we have and do the best we can with it, trusting in God implicitly. When we learn how to multiply little things with God's help, then He will be able to teach us to multiply bigger things. That leads back to humble beginnings.

The number or degree of gifts or talents we have does not make the difference. Trusting God to help us apply and multiply them makes all the difference.

An unforgettable example for me from the Bible is when God told Moses to go before Pharaoh. Moses asked, "Who am I, that I should go before Pharaoh and bring the Israelites out of Egypt?" Moses had but a cane and a confidence problem. Still, Moses took what little he had and put it to work for God. You know the rest of the story—the parting of the Red Sea, the Ten Commandments, leading the Israelites out of the wilderness, helping them find the Promised Land . . . Moses knew he wasn't capable of completing all these tasks on his own. But Moses finished big because he followed God's lead. He didn't give up, no matter how impossible things seemed, and he trusted God to make the way.

Take what you have been given, no matter how simple or insignificant it might seem to you, and use it for the Lord!

My brethren, count it all joy when you fall into various trials, knowing that the testing of your faith produces patience.

James 1:2-3

PART TWO

THE TRIALS

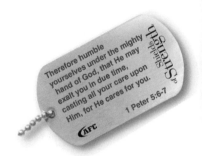

Therefore humble yourselves under the mighty hand of God, that He may exalt you in due time, casting all your care upon Him, for He cares for you.

1 Peter 5:6-7

CHAPTER THREE

THE COMPETITION

S kiing was quickly becoming more of a passion for me than a pastime. After that first summer, I found myself skiing as much as I fished.

I skied my first tournament at the age of eleven. That year, I remember going home with a friend one day after training. His name was Charlie Fontenot. I didn't know then that when we were older, Charlie would become my ski coach. (Charlie has been my coach now for more than fifteen years.)

While waiting in his living room that day, I was drawn to his trophy collection displayed there. A large medal shone from a glass shadow box hanging on the wall. I was mesmerized by it.

My friend explained to me that the object of my interest was a national competition medal and his most prized possession. At that very moment, I felt a dream rise up within my heart of one day winning a national championship competition and taking home such a medal or trophy of my own.

Little did I know to what heights and depths that dream would carry me. My path seemed clear to me. I could not know how much more God had planned for me. I thought I understood the prize, but God had set His sights on so much more for me.

Within a couple of years, I was skiing well enough to qualify for the state and regional ski tournaments. I was learning fast and moving up in the sport more quickly than most of my age-level competitors.

At the age of thirteen, I faced my first big setback when all of my competitors hit a growth spurt, and I seemed to have stopped growing. For the next three years, my success was hindered by the fact that I hardly grew an inch. Once a month my parents were driving me to Galveston, Texas, where specialists were monitoring my growth to determine if I would need growth hormones. The situation posed a heart-rending paradox. While I was striving my hardest to become a champion athlete, doctors were trying to determine if my body would continue to grow normally or if it had prematurely stopped growing.

By the time I was a sophomore in high school, I was but half the size of my competition. I felt I was living out the epic of David and Goliath on the waterfront and the ski circuit. Standing four feet, eleven inches tall, and weighing one hundred pounds, I was dwarfed by the other high school skiers.

I gained only an inch during my entire sopho-more year.

Barely five feet tall during my junior year, I skied well enough to qualify in the regional tournament as a favorite to place in the top three. That placement would qualify me for the national tournament, a benchmark in my dream quest. That was in 1983, and it would have been great if God had planned for me to win that year . . . but it wasn't to be. He had a longer, more arduous course set up for me, a course that would bring me closer to Him, and that would allow my ski trials to take on more meaning than I could ever imagine.

I mentioned earlier that the jump speed of a competition skier approaches sixty miles an hour. The jump climbs almost as high as a three-story building and the average distance spans three-fourths the length of a football field, or about seventy-five yards.

That year during the regional competition, on my first of three jumps, I came off the ramp with bad timing and worse position. Halfway through the jump, I had turned completely upside down. When I hit the water, my right ski hit my left ankle and slashed it open. Though I made my plea to the judges to continue with the competition, the judges ruled that the injury was too severe for me to continue.

For the Lord God will help me; therefore I will not be disgraced; therefore I have set my face like a flint, and I know that I will not be ashamed.

Isaiah 50:7

CHAPTER FOUR

SUCCESS NOSEDIVES

By the following summer, I had all but for-gotten the accident and was focused again on the regional tournament coming up in Baton Rouge, Louisiana. I spent the summer train-ing with all my heart. The discipline and hard work made a difference. A full month before the tournament, I was skiing better than the year before.

Coming into the regional competition, I was favored to place first or second, an easy quali-fier for the national tournament. But two weeks before the tournament, I took the biggest fall of my short career and broke my left femur (thigh bone) completely in two. I would spend two months in the hospital, the next two years getting the strength back in my leg, and another year catching up to the competition.

The summer of 1987—a full three years after the broken leg—I was back in shape and skiing better than ever. Every setback seemed to strengthen my resolve and equip me with a better understanding of the obstacles before me. Coming into the regional tournament that year in Dallas, Texas, I was at top performance and primed for the championship.

My first jump of the regional tournament was one of my best ever. I felt certain I would place first or second, and finally get my chance to compete at the national level.

Everything seemed perfect as I pushed off the ramp for the first jump. Then, at the peak of the jump, something went wrong. The tips of my skis dropped, allowing the wind to get on top of the skis. When that happened, both of the ski tips went straight down, immediately causing me to invert.

I landed hard on my back and shoulders, and the force of the fall knocked me unconscious. When the rescue swimmers reached me, I was floating face down in the water. As the rescue team lifted me up and over to get my face out of the water, I regained consciousness.

Somehow I was able to convince the judges I was fine to ski again. But before I could take another jump, I blacked out a second time. It was then, I guess, when I sort of blacked out on my faith, too.

Trust in the Lord with all your heart and lean not on your own understanding; in all your ways acknowledge Him; and He will make your paths straight.

Proverbs 3:5-6

CHAPTER FIVE

LETTING GO OF FAITH

After the injuries and blackouts, I started believing and accepting that I was a failure. Recounting my struggle up to that point, I saw that every time I reached the top of my game, I would make a poor decision, or something would happen to send my hopes plummeting. It seemed like I had been taking one step forward and two steps back. As discouragement settled over me, I began slowly to let go of my faith so gradually and subtly that, at first, I didn't realize what was happening.

When I headed for regionals the next year, I was skiing smarter and better than ever. But spiritually, I wasn't prepared to even get out of bed, much less tackle competition. Instead of expecting to win, I was focused on not failing. I skied without passion, joy, or resolve, shadowed by the fear that I would waste another opportunity.

That year I won the regionals, though I lived the triumph not as a victory, but as an extension of the fear that had flooded my spirit. Winning, when I was full of fear, was empty and more frightening, I think, than losing with a sound mind.

I can remember the national competition in 1988 as if it were yesterday. My good friend Trey Cox and I drove from Beaumont, Texas, to West Palm Beach, Florida, for the tournament. We drove twenty-three hours non-stop from Beaumont to West Palm Beach. I was scheduled to ski early the next morning. I experienced the adventure of the road trip, the fulfillment of a part of my dream, and the challenge ahead of me, not with elation and excitement, but with a growing sense of dread. I was enduring the event rather than embracing the opportunity. Every mile of the drive seemed to add to my fear of failure.

Once there, I joined more than a thousand of the nation's best skiers, most of them pumped and primed to win. I gauged my chances against the skiers I saw who were twice my size and who exhibited equal or better skills. Most had skied in several national competitions already. My mood sunk lower as my fear rose. I was sure I would lose . . . and so I did.

When the competition was over, I had been out-jumped by more than forty feet. I didn't wait for the results. I left the competition site before the tournament was even over, went back to the hotel, loaded up my luggage, and headed home. For ten years, I had fought for a chance to make my dream come true, but when I finally had the chance, I skied so poorly that no one even knew I had shown up.

There had been other losses in my ski career—more losses than wins. Many times I had been beaten in competition by greater degrees. But those disappointments proved to only strengthen my resolve to fight that much harder to win. This loss was a total defeat. This time I had not only lost the physical battle, I'd lost the spiritual trial as well by acting on fear instead of faith. The sense of failure was so deep and devastating for me that I felt totally defeated—and I completely gave up skiing.

CHAPTER SIX

TIME OUT

For the next five years, I never touched my skis. I took all my skiing gear and put it away where I would not have to look at it and be reminded that I had given up. I did what I could to avoid traveling the road that passed the water ski training lake. For the first couple of years, I still received my water ski magazines and other literature. I would always throw them away without looking them over. After two years off the water, I was doing fine and had done a good job of putting most of the memories out of my mind.

My only lingering problem came every August when the USA Water Ski Nationals were held. No one needed to tell me it was that time of year. I could feel it in the air. In the South, thunderstorms are very common in the heat of summer. Ski tournaments are often interrupted by storms and the lightning that comes with them. My fifth year out, I remember being on a trip to South Texas when I stopped for some gas on a desolate highway in the middle of nowhere. After starting the gas pump, I felt the summer heat and noticed a thunderstorm on the horizon. Until that point, I had been excited about the trip and did not even remember that the Water Ski Nationals were in progress.

The approaching storm suddenly reminded me of the championship ski competition underway. In that moment, I knew I was out of place and that I should be there. For the rest of the trip, I wrestled with my thoughts. Part of me really missed chasing my dream and wanted to think of being there and winning, but the other part wanted to just forget about it and have a good time on my trip.

In those five years of not skiing, my desire to win a national gold medal had not decreased even a little bit. The one thing that had decreased was my belief that I could win a national championship. Because I had ended on a fear high and saw my efforts and myself as a failure, I was convinced that I wasn't good enough to win the nationals.

I thought I would never ski again.

For we walk by faith not by sight.

AFC   II Corinthians 5:7

Shield of Strength®

CHAPTER SEVEN

TIME IN

By the summer of 1992, everything was looking down. I was five years removed from my chance at my dream, and I had just gone through a break up with a long-time girl friend. I was wondering where my life was going. After a Saturday of fishing, I was tired and feeling brokenhearted. Around 9:00 p.m. as I lay on my couch at my apartment, I heard a knock on the patio door. I answered the door and my little brother Gabe walked in all dressed up for a night on the town. He was all smiles, insisting I get up, get dressed, and go out with him and his friends.

I was positive that was not happening. I got back on the couch and said, "Thanks, but I am in no mood to leave."

For the next thirty minutes, he tried to coax me into going with him. I never even considered it. After about forty-five minutes, he went to the closet, pulled out one of my shirts, and got out my iron and ironing board. He brought them to the room I was in and started ironing a shirt for me. I told him I appreciated his thoughtfulness, but he was wasting his time. After he finished ironing the shirt and dousing my carpet with starch, he pulled out some white jeans, my cowboy hat, my boots, and a belt from my closet, and told me to fix my hair. After an hour, he was more determined than when he walked in the door. The more I said no, the more determined he became until I finally agreed to go with him, on one condition: as soon as I wanted to come home, we would come home.

We drove about an hour into Louisiana to a club called the Longhorn. When I figured out where we were going, I was really wishing I had stayed on the couch. Gabe was only trying to help me and did not want to see me home sulking and feeling sorry for myself, but this was looking like a bad idea and I was not feeling any better. Inside the club, everyone seemed to be having a great time. I took a seat on a bench in the middle of the crowd and wondered why I had ever agreed to come here. As I got up to find a quieter place out of the crowd, I saw my former girlfriend there dancing and having what looked to me like a great time. I was ready to leave! Only my little brother could get me into something like this. A few minutes later, I found him and told him I was ready to go. He started giving me his come-on-have-some-fun pitch and I let him know with some conviction I was ready to leave.

As we were about to walk out, a girl whom I had noticed earlier walked by us. I told Gabe to look at her, that I had seen her across the dance floor earlier that night and she seemed out of place. She was beautiful—or "fine" as we say in Southeast Texas. I was sure that she was too good looking to notice me, and she looked too proper for a stranger in a cowboy hat to approach. Besides, I was in no mood to talk to a girl anyway.

I should have never said all that to Gabe. He started pushing me her direction and urging me to ask her to dance. I told him the last thing I needed on my way out was for a girl to tell me she did not want to dance with me. The more I argued with him, the more adamant he was about my asking her to dance.

Finally, I made it real clear that I was leaving, not asking her to dance, and through with our conversation. Through, that is, until he told me that if I did not ask her to dance, he would. Now, I knew that Gabe has a way with the girls, and that if he asked her to dance, he would get that dance, so I told him to wait there. I went over to her and introduced myself. She told me her name was Tammie. I was expecting something like hello or good evening or some fancy greeting. When I asked her if she would like to dance, she said sure. The first song we danced was a slow song, and it was longer than usual because the song was played more than once. After that, we danced for four or five songs straight. By the end of the night, I had mustered enough courage to ask Tammie for her phone number, and also to ask her what she was doing the next day. She said she was going to the beach with some of her friends. Of course, I said, "So am I!" I got her phone number and she left. I saw Gabe a few minutes later, and the first thing he asked was if I had gotten the "digits," or phone number.

All the way home I was on cloud nine. Gabe and I went to the beach the next day, and it took all day for me to find Tammie and her friends. After a short visit, everyone was going home, so just before we all left, I asked her if she wanted to go to a movie. She took me up on the invitation and we went out with my sister and her boyfriend the next night. After the movie, I took Tammie home and we sat for hours on her parents' couch, talking about everything.

I didn't realize it that night, but Tammie was my soulmate, my future wife, and the person who would set my life back on track and open my head and my heart to how God would turn my trials to trophies for me and countless others struggling with their fear and their faith.

It wasn't long after Tammie and I started seeing each other on a regular basis and getting to know each other better, that the subject of my skiing came up. I was surely not going to tell her I had quit due to fear, so I told her I was just burned out. She asked me if she could see me ski, and I wanted to impress her. When I called my old ski coach, he told me to come on out and jump. It was that pride thing that had first gotten me up on the skis, to make sure I kept up with my sister, and I guess it was a bit of that pride that made me want Tammie to see me ski and jump. Many times fear follows closely on the heels of pride, and I would later have to turn that pride over to God in order to step free of the fear.

Anyway, one trip to the lake led to another, and before I knew it, I was skiing regularly again.

I had spent a lot of time in the gym during my ski-less five-year stint. The workouts had added twenty pounds of muscle to my frame. I was stronger than I had ever been, and the added strength improved my skiing. In three months, I was skiing at a level much higher than before I had quit.

Everything seemed to be going great. In an effort to keep the fear of failure from creeping in and taking over, I decided that if I did get to compete at nationals again, I would not expect to win. I thought that if I accepted the idea that I was not capable of winning, I would not have to worry about the fear of failing.

I must stop here and say this: never take that attitude! God only knows how many of His champions have lived their lives with this attitude stifling their potential, killing their dreams, and limiting God's plan for them.

I don't like to even mention the devil, because Scripture says he is already defeated through Christ, but I must say that adopting an attitude that embraces failure is the devil's greatest tool of deception. When you begin to believe that you can never become a champion, the devil won't come against you with fear. He doesn't need to, because you have already defeated yourself.

I compare this sad acceptance as similar to being under the rule of a tyrannical dictator who demands that his subjects accept poverty in order to be left in peace. Control by oppression and fear is cowardly, and is totally the opposite of all God has planned for our lives.

The Bible says: "The devil comes only to steal and to kill and destroy; I have come that you may have life, and have it more abundantly." John 10:10.

In Jeremiah 29:11, God says: "For I know the plans I have for you, plans to prosper you, not to harm you. Plans to give you a future and a hope."

How can we justify self-pride or fear when we read those statements?

When we can see our lives as more about God than about ourselves, it's kind of hard to concede defeat in any situation. A trial is just a footpath to walk with God. A challenge is just an opportunity to hold His hand more tightly. The element of loss is fleeting for those who walk in faith. We may not know how He will make it work, but if we have faith, we know He will make every setback work for our good if we follow His lead. Then we can consider adversity an incredible adventure with God.

> "And we know that God causes all things to work together for good to those who love God, to those who are called according to His purpose."
> —*Romans 8:28*

A new heart also will I give you, and a new spirit will I put within you.

AFC

Ezekiel 36:26

Shields of Strength

CHAPTER EIGHT

GIVING IT UP

My first year back, I placed third in the regionals again, and for the second time in my life, I qualified for nationals. But qualifying was about all I did. When I got to the national tournament in West Palm Beach, Florida, I couldn't help but hope that I would win at least a medal. But as soon as I decided to hope, I was suddenly reminded of all the fear and failure of my last national competition experience.

The night before the competition, I hardly slept. Every hour I would wake up to check the clock to see if it was time to get up and get ready to ski. Maybe this time I had a real chance to place in the top three. That hope wrestled with my fear of messing up again. The speed, skill, and timing called for in a national ski competition require a sound mind. A focus on fear overrides the possibility of a sound mind. In my performance that year, there was no question that hope lost the battle.

In short, I skied horribly. The performance wasn't the result of a bad break or chance circumstances, but of my conscious decision to act on fear. Both times that I had been given the chance to make my dream come true, I couldn't keep my wits about me long enough to follow through. I felt, each time, like I had thrown the dream overboard.

The worst realization to me was that I really didn't have the heart of a champion. I couldn't face the competition head on, couldn't rally to the challenge, and couldn't make my hard work, expertise, determination, and desire stand up against my fear. My perception was built on my control, not God's; on my potential and fallibility, not God's love and power and faithfulness; on my glory, not God's.

I learned that God can change hearts, if we let Him.

For we wrestle not against flesh and blood, but against principalities, against powers, and against the rulers of darkness of the world. Ephesians 6:12

CHAPTER NINE

TAKING IT BACK

The next year I had a plan. Through discipline, hard work, and mind power, I was going to beat the fear. I trained extra hard, skiing a minimum of five days a week. Tammie made sure that every training session I had was videotaped, and I reviewed my videos every night without fail. I would look for any missteps or mistakes, and visualize every way to make the jumps better, faster, farther.

That year at regionals in Austin, Texas, I won the competition. So far, the hard work and discipline were paying off. Still, I wanted to leave as little as possible to chance. I planned to arrive at the national tournament site, West Palm Beach again, two days early so I could practice on the lake and ramp. I figured the extra time would allow me to familiarize myself with my competition and the surroundings. Surely that would diminish my fear and anxiety.

Once at the competition site, I met the fear I had been trying to dodge. All the hard work, the discipline, and the careful plans didn't shield me from the fear. In fact, all my hard work did not even phase the fear. I felt more afraid than ever before.

That year, up to that point, I had skied for six months straight—more than six hundred jumps without a crash. But in Thursday's tournament practice, with fear robbing me of a sound mind, I crashed on my second jump. On Friday, I took to the lake for one last practice set, and I crashed on my first jump.

The following day was the day I would compete in the nationals, and Friday's practice proved a good predictor of how I would do in the competition.

My first two jumps were only 135 feet each, and though I had no certainty of how far my jumps were, I knew neither seemed good enough to win. When it came time for my last jump, I was in a total state of panic. I decided to forget about everything I had been taught to do, and on my last jump build as much speed as possible and attack the ramp with or without control. That mindset is one of the best ways to get hurt in my sport, and though I knew this in my heart, somehow the pain of an injury seemed easier to swallow than the humiliation and pain of fear and failure.

On that last jump I did everything wrong, but I did manage to keep from crashing. The jump was enough to put me in third place. But I knew I had skied poorly, and that I had moved through the competition that day as if I were living out a bad dream. It is a nightmare to be so totally without confidence and faith, and to be so consumed with such a smothering dread of failure.

In any struggle, a sense of progress strengthens hope. I can usually tell about how far I jump.

In the air I know if it's a good or bad jump, and on the landing I can usually judge if I've out-distanced the competition or jumped short. But after my last tournament jump that day, I had no idea how I had done. All year, I had been focused on every move, every position, every lean and landing, and every edge in every prac-tice session. Now, when it mattered most of all, the fear was taking away my judgment, my focus, and any sense of progress. My hope had been shoved out once again by fear.

Even though I took home the bronze that year, I knew I had skied poorly in a heavy cloak of fear that weighed me down, kept me from doing the best I could do, and robbed me of any joy in winning.

I remember walking away from the lake, still wrapped up in my fear, as the US team coach approached me to tell me that my last jump had moved me into third place. I told him, "Jay, I need to come ski with you. I need some help bad." And even though Jay Bennett is the finest ski jump coach I know, the truth was that something was pulling me down, something that physical train-ing and technique couldn't counter.

Physical training and preparation are a must, and I would not have had a chance, with or with-out the fear, if I had not trained so hard. Still, it was becoming clear that physical might was no match for the battle I was fighting against fear and failure. Gradually, I was beginning to understand that I needed more than physical training to win, and the battle I was losing was a spiritual battle.

Don't throw away your confidence; it will be richly rewarded.

AFC   Hebrews 10:35

Shield of Strength

CHAPTER TEN

Persevering

In 1996, I would qualify again for nationals, by skiing the best I had ever skied. In most of my practice sets, I was jumping far enough already to win the national tournament.

Tammie had seen the fear I was fighting. She knew the fear never left me when I skied. She also knew that I needed to learn that God's word, not my hard work, would get me through the fear. Tammie and her mom were strong Christians who knew God's word, and knew how to pray. They both understood spiritual battles.

I loved the Lord but I did not know His word, and I did not believe I should be asking the Lord for anything unless it meant life or death.

I remember Tammie and her mom inviting me to church one Wednesday night. It was a nice little church in Tammie's hometown of Nederland, Texas. When the service started, everything seemed normal enough to me. Then, about halfway into the worship time, I noticed that some people started getting a little excited. The churches I had always attended were very formal, and I had come to regard that formality as respectful to the Lord.

After another three or four songs, I saw a few more folks getting carried away, and jumping up and shouting. Before long, I was feeling very uncomfortable, like I needed to take control, get things back in order, and let these people know that this was the Lord's house and they should show a little more respect. About then I looked over at Mrs. Roccaforte (Tammie's Mom) and she was grinning from ear to ear. I did not want to offend Mrs. Roccaforte, so I kept my mouth shut and endured the service. I was very glad when it was over.

Later, at home, I thought about Tammie and her mom, both of whom I considered sound-minded people. Why would they be attending a church like that? I needed to talk to someone about it, so the next day I called my uncle Richard. I didn't really know Uncle Richard very well because the only times I ever talked to him were at Thanksgiving each year. But he was the pastor of the family, and I thought I could tell him about the service, and perhaps get him to tell me what was wrong with those people. I told my uncle about the whole church trip, and he invited me over for a steak so we could get into the Bible and see what it said. That sounded great to me.

I believed the Bible was God's word, and I wanted to know what it had to say about all this. I made the trip and Uncle Richard spent about two hours with me just showing me Scriptures and what the Bible said about praying, praising, and the presence of the Lord. He made certain I had received Jesus as my Savior.

Tammie and I started attending his church the very next Sunday. I knew I had a lot to learn, and that it was going to take a while.

Most of that year I prayed God would help me with my fear. I quoted Scriptures constantly. I was trying to get in shape spiritually. Uncle Richard, Tammie, and Mrs. Roccaforte were doing a good job of teaching me how to develop a relationship with the Lord, how to learn and apply His word, and how to listen to the Lord. I was doing everything I knew how to do to overcome my fear of ski competition, including praying while I skied. Nothing seemed to make a difference.

As the weeks moved me closer to the competition, Tammie continued to watch me struggle incessantly with my fear. In order to help me, Tammie wrote two Scriptures on my water ski tow handle: "I can do all things through Christ who strengthens me," Philippians 4:13; and "For God has not given me the spirit of fear but of power, of love and of a sound mind." II Timothy 1:7.

At the three-week countdown before the national championship, I knew I was skiing well enough to win, but the fear was still shadowing me. In my heart, I didn't really want to work so hard, only to fail again. The thought of sleepless nights added to the fear. In desperation, I finally called my pastor and poured my soul out to him. I told him about the overwhelming fear and my deep desire to win. He prayed with me, and I continued to pray and train for the next two weeks.

For God has not
given me the spirit of
fear; but of power, of
love, and of a sound
mind.

II Timothy 1:7

Shields of Strength

AFC

CHAPTER ELEVEN

No Fear

A week before the 1996 national tournament, my mood was down and anxiety manifested itself as a constant lump in my throat and knot in my stomach. As I was driving home from practice one day that week, I felt a tremendous need to get out from under the pressure, the fear, and the dread. I came to the conclusion that I should just give up completely and accept that I could not overcome the fear. I felt I had done everything I knew how to do, but I hadn't gained any ground on controlling the fear. It had been a long, hard-fought, grueling battle. But I was just too weary and discouraged to go on fighting it. I needed to face the fact that I wasn't capable of overcoming the fear.

I realize now that acceptance would have set me on a path to be fearful, discouraged, and disheartened for life. Acceptance would have eaten away at my faith, little by little, and gradually destroyed any sense of self-worth in me.

I was mulling over all these thoughts as I was driving. And as soon as I gave in to failure and defeat—the very moment I accepted the lie that fear had finally beaten me and I was helpless against it—God spoke to me. It had never happened before and has not happened since. I believe God guides me daily, but not always like this! I did not hear a sound at all with my ears. God was speaking to my mind and my heart, and I knew the thoughts were not my own. As He was speaking to me, He was virtually changing my way of thinking, and He was redesigning my perspective about my self, my life, and my God.

To the best of my memory this is what He said: "Kenny, you are not incapable. You are a son of the King of Kings." (The Bible says that when we receive God, He gives us sonship. Anyone who has made a decision to receive Jesus as Lord and Savior then becomes a son or daughter of God.)

Next, He said: "Here is your problem: you constantly pray and quote Scripture, but my word says that whatever you ask according to my will, if you believe, you will receive it as yours."

I knew it was not God's will for me to have fear. II Timothy told me that.

Then God said this: "Now if you believe in me, you must believe in my word. If you ask and believe you receive, you have received. Your whole problem is that you pray and quote Scripture before you ski, while you are skiing, and after you ski—but you are not acting on that Scripture. What you are really doing is looking back over your shoulder to see if I am with you."

"If you really believe in my word, you will pray once, thank me for the answer, and then go out and do the best you can for me, knowing that I am with you. It is then that my will can be done, and you will never fail."

He also told me to change the way I prayed. Instead of asking Him for power, love, and a sound mind, He said to ask once, then every time after that to thank Him for what I had asked. I changed my prayer from asking to this:

"Lord, I thank you that you have not given me the spirit of fear, but of power, of love, and of a sound mind. I thank you that I can do all things through Christ who strengthens me. I thank you for your divine wisdom and your guardian angels. Now with this power, with this love, and with this sound mind, I will do the best I can for you so that your will can be done."

And right there, driving down I-10 in my truck, I realized my fear had been taken away. After fifteen years of fighting the fear, in the process of completely giving in and giving up, God delivered me.

I cast down imaginations, and every high thing that exalteth itself against the knowledge of God, and bring into captivity every thought to the obedience of Christ.

II Corinthians 10:5

Shields of Strength

AFC

CHAPTER TWELVE

THE STARTING DOCK

T he next week's training went very well, and by the end of that week I was headed for Fort Walton Beach, Florida, for the national championship competition. Tammie and I drove this trip since it was only about an eight-hour drive. She was supposed to help me stay awake on the trip, but Tammie cannot stay awake in a car, so she was sleeping before we crossed the Louisiana state line. She asked me to wake her up at each state line so she could see the welcome signs on the highway. When we made Louisiana, I woke her up, and she looked up for a minute, said, "Thank you, and make sure you wake me up when we get to the next state line."

I thought, *I guess that means I am driving this one alone.* When we got to Mississippi, I woke her up, and she again looked up, slurred a thank you, said she was sorry, and went right back to sleep. When we crossed into Alabama, she did the same thing. Finally, when we crossed the Florida state line, she felt so bad for sleeping the whole way she managed to stay awake for the last hour of the drive. I think she just wanted to see the beaches.

This would not be a year I would spend much time taking in the tournament talk at the starting dock. The starting dock at a ski tournament is like the water cooler in the office. The starting dock provides a tournament forum for the country's best skiers to share their opinions of the tournament conditions and to hash out problems with their practices.

At nationals, the conversation shared at the starting dock can be valuable and useful. Sometimes, though, the dialogue takes a downturn as folks make excuses for not overcoming their fears. I have been known to indulge in this kind of conversation myself, but often, in years past, I had found the discussions more distracting than beneficial.

The conversation usually goes something like this:

"Man, that boat driver is horrible!"

"The wind is up one minute and down the next..."

"The ramp is so fast you can't keep your balance!"

"That water is so slow it kills your timing."

"That boat makes a huge wake."

"They must have just put on a new rope. It's like a rubber band."

"The sun is a killer coming in to the ramp!"

And so on ...

That year, I felt my energy would best be spent in prayer, practice, and action—focusing on God's word and my training—rather than hanging around the starting dock. I had trained for every condition, and I was not going to sit around and listen to things that would distract me or fill me with fear. If there really was a problem, I would know it, and with a sound mind, I could adjust for it.

I share this because no matter what you do, you can find a "starting dock," where everybody who knows everything about what you do can share an endless string of negative comments that present problems without proposed solutions.

I say: Find a good starting dock buzzing with talk about overcoming, never giving up, and never failing through Christ. When this is the conversation around the water ski starting dock, I hang around. Apart from the ski competition circuit, good starting docks for life's challenges can exist in good churches and with good Christian friends and fellowship.

But seek ye first the
kingdom of God, and
His righteousness; and
all these things shall be
added unto you.

AFC

Matthew 6:33

Shields
of Strength

CHAPTER THIRTEEN

No Way to Lose

The next day was the big day. The same old
challenges began to line up like skiers in
a competition. Sleeping that night offered the
usual struggle for a short time, but then I managed to get to sleep and to sleep through the
night. I woke up early and felt well rested.

At the waterfront, my warm-up went smoothly.
I would be skiing as the fifth seed, or fifth from
the last contender in the line of sixty or so jump-
ers. The number-one-ranked skier competes
last in the lineup, so that meant there were only
four skiers ranked higher than I was.

During the day I had to choke back my fear several times. Tammie was by my side the whole

time, and she kept reminding me to stay focused on God's word. Over and over, she kept telling me she knew I would do well. She made it very clear she believed in me and felt the Lord was with me. Each time fear came creeping into my thoughts, I would focus on God's word, but I was still battling. II Corinthians 10:5 says: "Cast down imaginations and every high thing that exalts itself against the knowledge of God and bring into captivity every thought to the obedience of Christ." In other words, even though God had delivered me from my fear, it did not mean that I would not be tempted to be fearful again and again. The key to keeping my sound mind was to keep casting down negative and distracting thoughts, and to continue thinking on God's word instead.

When the lineup was down to the top ten skiers, I knew I was still in the running because no one had beaten my personal best. A skier's rank is based solely on his average performance in a certain number of tournaments. Sometimes, skiers have a few bad tournaments and end up ranked lower than they should be. All the top athletes know each other and we know who is skiing the best, regardless of ranking. That day I knew that if anyone would jump farther than I could, it would be Lyle, the skier skiing just before me. But when he had made two of his three jumps, he still had not taken over the lead. As he took his last jump, I was putting on my knee brace. I heard him hit the ramp, and then I heard the crowd break out in excited cheers and loud applause. As I put on the rest of my equipment, I heard his distance being announced. He had taken over first place with a 173-foot jump, and that was five feet farther than I had ever jumped.

Tammie helped me pull my speed suit on before she left to video my jumps and watch from a closer viewpoint. After hearing Lyle's distance, she told me I could do all things through Christ who strengthens me. She told me she knew I could do it and not to worry about how far Lyle jumped because she knew I could jump farther.

As I pulled my skis on, I started to think, *I can't believe it! I am one jump away from being able to take over the lead and maybe have my dream come true, and this guy jumps five feet farther than my personal best.*

Those thoughts seemed to bring the fear back in full force. But at that moment, I remembered II Timothy 1:7: "For God has not given me the spirit of fear, but of power, of love, and of a sound mind." I knew I needed to concentrate harder on God's word.

Then I had this thought: *I am just going to do the best I can for Jesus and not worry about winning.* I knew if I did the best I could for the Lord, He would be happy with me. As I made that decision, I realized that I would do more for the Lord than I would for a gold medal or trophy anyway.

It was some time after that fateful day that I found the Scripture for what God was telling me then, in Matthew 6:33: "But seek you first the kingdom of God and His righteousness and all these things will be added unto you."

In all things I am
more than a
conqueror through
Christ who loves me.
Romans 8:37

CHAPTER FOURTEEN

NO WAY TO WIN

My first jump was 172 feet—four feet farther than my personal best but still one foot short of the leader. On my second attempt, my timing was off. As I finished making my turn for the final approach to the ramp, I realized I was running behind and I might not get on the ramp. The closer I got to the ramp, the more it looked like I might miss it. In that situation, I know to let go of the rope, and ski around to avoid hanging my skis on the side of the ramp. But because I wanted to win so badly, I did not let go of the rope.

I felt my right ski hang on the side of the ramp. That threw me off balance. I lost control and crashed. Both skis came off in the water.

I wasn't hurt, but when I came to rest in the water, I could see I had ripped the fin off the bottom of my right ski. I always carry a spare fin and a battery-powered hand screwdriver for such an emergency. In ski competition, a skier has three minutes to repair any kind of equipment damage or failure. If the repairs are not finished within the three minutes, the judges call a forced forfeit.

The boat rushed me back to the starting dock where I could replace the broken fin with a new one. Working as quickly as I could, I managed to secure the new fin. As soon as I had the last screw tightened, I heard the judge's voice over the boat radio announcing that my time was up. I let them know immediately that I was ready, and hurriedly began to put my skis back on. I pulled my left ski on first. Then as I slid my foot into the right ski, I noticed the boot felt way too loose. Tight boots allow a skier more control. Competition skiers wear their ski boots so tight they have to lubricate them with soap to even slide their feet into them.

My heart dropped when I saw that the right boot was torn. I hadn't noticed it after the crash because my skis had come off during the fall. Now, there was no more time for repairs. The boat took off and I was up and on my way to set up for my third and final jump of the competition.

These thoughts crowded my consciousness and colored the remainder of the day hopelessly dark: *It's over. I did my best, and I almost made it. At least I can probably count on having second place wrapped up . . . I overcame my fear and jumped four feet farther than my personal best. But now my concentration is broken, and, worst of all, my boot is torn. I'll have to settle for second place because there is no way I can make the jump I need to win with a torn boot. No one can do that.*

The boat was making its final turn to start the approach to the ramp when the Lord reminded me that I had committed to do the best I could for Him. I knew that until I had taken that third and final jump, I had not finished doing the best I could for the Lord. No matter what the circumstances and regardless of the torn boot—I could still do my best until I was finished.

As I headed for the ramp, I remembered the Scripture on my ski rope handle, the Scripture Tammie had written there to help me overcome my fear. Yes, I can do all things through Christ who strengthens me. Okay, then.

I would continue on with a clear head and do the best I could with the torn boot. If I were out of control, I could refuse the ramp, let go of the rope and ski around, but at least I would have acted on God's word until I finished.

But things got worse. When I made my first cut to set up my approach to the ramp, I cut out too soon. It is very hard to start out too early or too late and make all the corrections I need to make in order to get my timing right before I hit the ramp. If I can't correct a too-early start, I won't have enough speed to make a long jump.

Any other time before that day, I know I would have panicked at my poor timing on such a critical jump, even without the torn boot. But this time I remember matter-of-factly thinking that I knew how to correct the situation. To get my timing on track, I needed to make a long slow turn and pull as hard as I could to get farther past the boat. I remember that as I pulled up beside the boat, I was riding my skis as flat as possible and staying as low as possible, trying to delay my timing.

As I made my final turn to the ramp, I knew all my weight would be on my right ski—the ski with the torn boot. In order to prevent my foot from slipping, I shoved my foot to the right side of the boot and kept constant pressure on that foot all the way to the ramp.

It seemed that each small wave, wind, lean, motion, and movement on my part was critical. All the odds were against me even completing this jump. Odds were great that I would be injured, and odds were almost nil that this last jump could possibly be a winning jump.

I knew that if I eased up or bounced on the water at all, my foot would slip. And I knew that in order to adjust my timing, I needed to execute the turn . . . slower . . . slower . . . but not too slow. . . . As I finished the turn, I sensed my timing was still too early. From the completion of the last turn until I make contact with the ramp it is only about three seconds. In those three seconds, my speed accelerates from about ten miles an hour to almost sixty miles an hour.

PART THREE

THE TROPHY

We will shout for joy when you are victorious and will lift up our banners in the name of our God.   Psalms 20:5

AFC

Shield of Strength

CHAPTER FIFTEEN

THE VICTORY

In the past, I would have totally succumbed to the fear and lost my sound mind. All my logical reasoning told me that my last jump was doomed for failure. My poor timing and speed were odds enough against me. The torn boot alone would make a winning jump impossible. All three factors combined set up odds too stiff for anyone to overcome.

But within the critical three seconds—as the boat shot me forward to sixty miles an hour— the unthinkable, unlikely, impossible began to take hold. With as clear and as sound a mind as I had ever had, I was able to tap into everything I had learned over my years of training. I took as long as I could in the turn without taking too long. I was still too early, so I started slowly and pulled harder as I approached the ramp. Halfway to the ramp I knew that I had finally gotten my timing on track, but that I did not have enough speed. I pulled as hard as I could to generate as much speed as possible, while also making sure I kept my right foot shoved hard into the right side of the torn boot.

When I reached the ramp, I was sure I still did not have enough speed, and I knew I would need to kick the ramp as hard as I could to get extra height and make up for the loss of speed. I executed the kick and timing perfectly, and I am certain that God performed a miracle at that point, because I went straight up without slipping one bit.

Sailing through the air, halfway through the jump, I realized that my dream had just come true. My last jump was 179 feet—eleven feet farther than my personal best and distance enough to win the nationals by six feet.

After I got my skis off, I took off running to find Tammie in the crowd near the jump. When

I found her, she was crying. She hugged me and told me how proud she was of me. I asked her what was wrong, and she said she had been strong in front of me, but when she walked away to go video my jumps, she had started crying. She said she was afraid for me because she knew I would have to jump so far to win. She said she knew I could do it, but she was worried I wouldn't. She had been crying and praying the whole time. I could not wait to tell her what had been happening in my heart during that competition.

As we began the long drive home, I began sharing with Tammie how the Lord had been working in my spirit as I struggled through those three jumps, and how much boldness He had given me. Before we got to the Florida state line, I noticed she was not responding. I left her alone and let her sleep the whole way. I did not need any help to stay awake. I wore my gold medal the whole way home. I relived everything a hundred times and cried every time. I thanked the Lord so many times for all He had done for me. Another thing became very clear to me on my way home and that was that I would need Tammie in my life forever.

I started saving for a ring and December 24, 1996, I told Tammie I wanted her to come to church with me and go to the altar so we could pray together and thank God for everything that had happened that year. Uncle Richard opened up the church, and we went and prayed together at the altar. When she got up, I stayed on my knees and asked her to be my wife. She accepted, thank God, and we were married the following May.

CHAPTER SIXTEEN

IN VICTORY'S WAKE

I am here to tell you that overcoming fear is about making a conscious decision to think and act on God's word. Yes, I did need my physical preparation and all the training. Physically, I was prepared, and that was very important. However, until I got spiritually prepared, I could never have accomplished my dream. All the physical training in the world cannot help you overcome a spiritual battle with fear. But God has already overcome fear for us if we will simply act on His word in any and all circumstances.

When I made a decision to act on God's word spiritually, I picked up the shield of faith and the sword of the spirit, which enabled me to function with a sound mind. Ephesians 6 says it like this:

"Be strong with the Lord's mighty power. Put on all of God's armor so that you will be able to stand firm against all strategies and tricks of the devil. For we are not fighting against people made of flesh and blood, but against the evil rulers and authorities of the unseen world, against those mighty powers of darkness who rule this world, and against wicked spirits in the heavenly realms. Use every piece of God's armor to resist the enemy in the time of evil, so that after the battle you will be standing firm. Stand your ground, putting on the sturdy belt of truth and the body armor of God's righteousness. For shoes, put on the peace that comes from the Good News, so that you will be fully prepared. In every battle you will need faith as your shield to stop the fiery arrows aimed at you by Satan. Put on salvation as your helmet, and take the sword of the spirit, which is the word of God. Pray at all times and on every occasion in the power of the Holy Spirit."

What I learned has made a difference in how I have lived each day since. The truth is that my fear was never a physical problem. It was a spiritual problem. My fear was coming from an evil power in some high place. Putting it plainly and simply, the devil was trying to prevent me from functioning with a sound mind. Recognizing the real battle was one critical step for me. Understanding how to fight it was another.

For years, I fought the fear with my own effort until I could not fight anymore. Then I gave up, but fortunately God did not give up on me, and the solution was much simpler than I had ever dreamed. All I had to do was act on God's word, no matter my circumstances. If you think about it, every time the devil tempted the Lord, Jesus would simply quote Scripture, and the devil would flee. I figured if Jesus used God's word to run off the devil, then so should I. However, just quoting Scripture is not enough on its own. It wasn't until I decided to act on God's word that I overcame my fear.

The good news is that we do not have to fight Satan. All we need to do is what God has already told us to do in Ephesians 6—we need to pick up the shield of faith and the sword of the spirit. As I said before, in II Corinthians 10:5, the Scripture says we should cast down imaginations and every high thing that exalts itself against the knowledge of God and bring into captivity every thought to the obedience of Christ. This Scripture is talking about the same high thing, and God is telling us that to overcome the devil, all we need to do is cast out of our minds thoughts of fear, and act on God's word.

The next question is: What are "thoughts obedient to Christ?" The answer can be found in Philippians 4:8, which reads: "Finally, brothers, whatever is true, whatever is noble, whatever is right, whatever is pure, whatever is lovely, whatever is admirable—if anything is excellent or praiseworthy—think about such things. Whatever you have learned or received or heard from me, or seen in me—put it into practice. And the God of peace will be with you."

Now, when I am struck with a thought or thoughts that do not line up with what God's word says, I make a conscious decision to think and act, not on those thoughts, but on God's word instead. I continue striving to make decisions based on what God says, not what circumstances or the devil might lead me to think. I do this because I have realized God's word is good for me and is truer than anything I see or feel anyway.

Leading up to those final moments at the national competition, all I could feel in my heart and hear in my mind was defeat. Looking at my situation, defeat was the only outcome that made sense. But by faith, I decided to act on God's word. When I did that, I allowed God to work in me to overcome my circumstances. As a result, I found that the truth was God's word; simply said, He had not given me the spirit of fear, but of power, of love, and of a sound mind. I can do all things through Christ who strengthens me. Don't try to do this with the power of positive thinking. Positive thinking is great, but it is not the sword of the spirit or the shield of faith. Positive faith in God can provide you the sword and shield and can make an absolute difference.

When I had only one jump left, everything seemed to be going wrong for me, and the negative thoughts kept pressing into my consciousness. I see now that these thoughts were the fiery darts of the devil trying to coax me to act on those thoughts. God says that with every temptation, He will provide the way of escape. After these thoughts went through my mind, God reminded me that I had committed to do the best I could for Him. He also reminded me of Philippians 4:13. This was my way of escape, but I had to put the Scripture into action and act on the Scripture.

Hebrews 11:1 says: "Faith is the substance of things hoped for and the evidence of things not seen."

James 2:17 says: "Faith without action is dead." Looking back, it is easy for me to see that I was going to win the nationals if I just acted on God's word.

I once heard a man say that fear is **F**alse **E**vidence **A**ppearing **R**eal. I'll buy that! God does not want us to be moved by what we see or hear, but to be moved only by His word. When I acted on God's word, I found the truth.

As for God, His way is perfect; the word of the Lord is proven; He is a shield to all who trust in Him.

Psalms 18:30

CHAPTER SEVENTEEN

SHIELDS OF STRENGTH

After winning the national championship, I found that what I had learned about fear also applies to my everyday life, and to challenges far more important than winning a medal or a trophy. Good examples are the challenges of being a good husband and a good father. At times, I would fear letting Tammie or my family down so much that when I heard one of them complain about anything, I would over-react in anger to the fear and to them. Another big fear for me was failing on the job. Many times, that fear has actually hindered my job performance. In family and career challenges, I realize that fear moves me toward the very realities that I fear.

I wanted a daily reminder of God's word, but figured I would look silly carrying my water ski tow rope handles with me wherever I went. So I bought a few military dog tags and engraved the Scriptures that I have mentioned on them. I wore them under my shirt as daily reminders for me.

Each time I would be tempted with fear or anger or anything else that would hinder me, I would read my II Corinthians tag that says: "I cast down imaginations and every high thing that exalts itself against the knowledge of God and bring into captivity every thought to the obedience of Christ."

Next I would read II Timothy 1: "For God has not given me the spirit of fear, but of power, of love, and of a sound mind." I found that what I had learned in winning the national championship could also help me win in life.

Over the next few months, I got several requests for the tags. Soon, my little brother started calling the necklaces Shields of Strength. And from a couple of small mementos, God has opened the door to heaven for hundreds of thousands of believers.

On the back of almost every Shield of Strength is inscribed the prayer we call the prayer of salvation. Prayers don't save anyone or get anyone to heaven, but a sincere decision to receive Jesus as your Lord and Savior will. Jesus said that anyone who comes to Him, He will not cast out. The Bible says that He stands at the door of our hearts, knocking, and He comes into the heart of anyone who will ask Him.

The Shields of Strength are reminders of God's love, power, and faithfulness, and an encouragement to act on His word instead of fear.

Kenny with his first bass.

Kenny learns to ride at an early age.

Kenny's father in his twenties.
Kenny later learned to jump at the same ski club.

The Vaughan children learning to jump.
(From top: Bonnie, Kenny, and Gabe)

FROM TRIALS . . .

TO TROPHIES!

Kenny poses with Dan Coufal, the
official announcer at the 1996 Nationals
in Fort Walton Beach, Florida.

Kenny celebrates with his wife Tammie
and long-time coach Charlie after
winning the gold medal.

As a National champion, Kenny is asked to speak about his experiences across the country.

Where it all began . . . pictured here is the tow rope handle that Tammie inscribed with the Scripture that inspired Kenny to act on his faith to win the gold medal above. Also pictured is the broken fin that nearly cost Kenny his dream and that he now keeps as a trophy.

Kenny's parents, Robert and Alice Vaughan

Kenny with his family.
From left to right: Faith, Kenny, Tammie, and Grace.

Dad shows Faith the ropes.

Kenny gears up at the starting dock.

Kenny takes a break from another long day of training.

Coach Charlie takes on his newest student, Faith.

Lieutenant Colonel Dodd poses with his wife Sharon and two daughters, Caitlin and Grace, before departing for Afghanistan.

Lieutenant Colonel Dean Triebel gave his last Shield of Strength to Oliver North, when this picture was taken in Iraq.

Major General Hylton gives Kenny a
Coin of Excellence for donating Shields
of Strength to Maj. Hylton's soldiers
before they deployed to Afghanistan.

The members of the 86th Signal Battalion pictured
here with their Shields of Strength were among
the first troops deployed to Afghanistan.

Lieutenant Colonel Dodd, Secretary of the Army
Les Brownlee, Kenny, and Lieutenant Colonel Joe
Rippetoe at the Pentagon.

Captain Russel Rippetoe—homecoming king, Eagle Scout, captain of the football team, Army Ranger, and Iraqi war hero—was killed in action on April 3rd, 2003.

He is pictured here (center) with his family.

Secretary of the Army Les Brownlee looks at Captain Russel Rippetoe's Bible, dog tags, Shields of Strength, and a note from Capt. Rippetoe's father.

All of these items were with Capt. Rippetoe when he was killed in action. Picture taken at the Pentagon.

After losing a comrade and close friend in battle,
Lance Corporal Chris Hankins is baptized in a
makeshift basin of plastic-covered boxes
wearing a Shield of Strength.

A memorial for nine marines and one translator is a
silent reminder of the price of freedom.

10th Mountain Division
United States Army

2002 USA
Waterski Nationals

National Aeronautics and
Space Administration

Special Warfare
Group 2 Navy Seals

All for One
United States Army

1st Infantry Division
United States Army

25th Infantry Division
United States Army

1st Cavalry Division
United States Army

United States Army

US Nuclear Security

75th Ranger Regiment
3rd Ranger Battalion
United States Army

82nd Airborne Division
United States Army

Firefighter Shield

Unit Ministry Team
3rd Infantry Division

US Naval Academy
Headquarters

Walter Reed Army
Medical Center

86th Signal Battalion
United States Army

Camp Willow Run

3rd Infantry Division
United States Army

The shields pictured here were custom made. For
more information about Shields of Strength or to
request a catalog, go to www.shieldsofstrength.com.

That the trial of your faith, being much more precious than gold that perisheth, though it be tried by fire, might be found unto praise and honor and glory at the appearing of Jesus Christ.

I Peter 1:7

CHAPTER EIGHTEEN

FROM TRIALS TO TROPHIES

I must add a closing chapter to this story, a chapter I believe holds many of the most important thoughts in this book's message.

That day in 1996 at the national competition, after I was awarded my gold medal, I was standing alone by the lake. Almost everyone had left, and I had time to myself to reflect and relive the moments of the day. While thinking back on my last jump, I remembered taking off the remainder of the fin that broke when I hung my ski on the side of the ramp. And I remembered throwing it on the ground so I could quickly replace it with the new fin. I decided to walk back to the starting dock to see if I could find the broken fin. I saw it still lying where I had tossed it, so I picked it up and took it home with me as a souvenir of the day.

After a few months, I came to realize that I treasured that broken fin about as much as I treasured my gold medal. I consider that fin a trophy. If I had given up and not acted on God's word, I would never have wanted to see that fin again. Today, I would give up my medal before I would part with that broken fin. For a while that seemed very strange to me. After all, that broken fin nearly prevented me from accomplishing my dream.

Now, I see it as trials to trophies. What I have learned is the devil wants the opposite. If the devil has his way, he will discourage us with fearful thoughts and keep us from acting on God's word during a time of trial. If Satan can keep us from acting on God's word, and persuade us to act on fear instead, we will fail, and the trial will become the devil's trophy. I believe the devil wants the trophy so he can remind us of our failures for the rest of our lives, and hinder us from benefiting the Kingdom of God.

I didn't realize it at the time, but when I quit skiing for those five years, I gave my trophy to the devil. He waved it in my face, constantly using it to make me believe I should not dream big about anything because I might fail and suffer the pain of failing again.

It's important to note that I did not give the devil my trophy when I lost at the nationals. I gave him my trophy when I acted on fear and quit fighting. Where you finish has nothing to do with winning your spiritual battle. Acting on God's word and doing the best you can for Him until you are finished, determines your spiritual victory.

Even if I had not finished first, I still would have considered my broken fin a trophy because I acted on God's word, doing the best I could for Him, and I did not quit until I was finished. Now that the trophy is mine, I am encouraged in everything I do, knowing that with Jesus, I can do anything. I see how He moved me through the trials to receive the trophies.

Many times in life, people and things act against us to try to prevent us from accomplishing our dreams. The truth is God's word that says: "We can do all things through Christ who strengthens us." The trials simply determine the depth of our character and the value of our testimony when we have done all things through Christ who strengthens us. God could have given me a national championship at the age of fourteen. After all, He is God. However, had I not faced all these trials, I would not be writing this book, I would not have made the first Shield of Strength, and I would have little to offer anyone.

Let me take this opportunity to tell you, straight out, to avoid the trials you can avoid without losing sight of your dreams. When you can't avoid a trial without losing sight of your dreams, roll up your sleeves, tell Katie to bar the door, spend some time praying, spend some time reading God's word, and then fight with power, love, and a sound mind, until God delivers you.

The cross was the greatest trial the world ever faced, yet today that cross is truly the world's greatest trophy. Thank God, Jesus followed through with his journey to the cross.

Always remember—the greater the trial, the greater the trophy!

Epilogue

Now, a few years later, I am still trying to win my second National Championship. I won the bronze at the Nationals in 2003. That day I was skiing with so much boldness and confidence, I went for a huge jump and the win. I hit a perfect jump and did exactly what I wanted to do, but I forgot to make sure I kept the sound mind part going when I underestimated and failed to adjust for a strong tail wind. That was my only crash all year, but the force of the fall broke a bone in my foot, a Liz Franc injury, that was difficult to heal and required surgery. Everything would have been great if there had not been that strong tail wind. Another lesson learned. Never stop asking God for wisdom. As soon as you get too confident, you go out on your own and hit a brick wall.

I was recovering well, but got off to a late start for the 2004 season. However, I didn't plan on letting that stop me from winning. I'd been skiing better than ever against much younger skiers who were raising the bar. The most amazing part is that I have skied with that same boldness the Lord gave me at the Nationals in 1996, for every tournament since, no matter how tough the competition or what I've had thrown at me.

I was looking forward to Nationals 2004. The competition was in West Palm Beach, where the whole fear thing started. I couldn't wait to go back and ski that site with the boldness Christ had given me.

Two days before I would fly out for the Nationals, another trial presented itself. During one of my last practices of the season, I crashed while landing a jump. According to the x-rays, I'd broken the ulna in my right arm. The doctors told me that the break would not require surgery, and with God's blessing, I believe it should heal 100 percent. I'm looking forward to what God has for me in the coming year, and can't wait to get back into competition, going to Nationals, and, with His grace, winning.

Training time will be a bit harder to come by. Tammie and I had our second daughter. Grace Ann Vaughan was born on March 1, 2004. Her big sister, Faith Elice Vaughan is four years older and learned to ski the summer of 2004. Her grandfather (my dad) took a sheet of plywood and cut a circle out for her and painted it the same color as the first one I rode. She started on the round disk I learned to ride when I was a boy, and a few months later she got up on skis. She likes to ride in the boat while I work on my jumps. She claps the whole time, and when I am finished working out for the day, she always tells me, "You did so good! I am proud of you, Daddy!"

Grace is just happy to see the sunshine, smile into our faces, and speak gibberish to anyone who stops to listen.

My prayer is that my children will see, through my life, an example of true faith and confidence in a Heavenly Father that is always there, who disciplines and guides with love, grace, and mercy, and knows the plan He has for each one of us.

Tammie still videos all my training sessions and has become quite a good skier herself. More than that, she is a wonderful wife and mom.

I am blessed with what God has shown me and how he is using my struggles to bring others closer to Him. I am thankful for each day, and for the way He has taught me to view the tests that life presents to me. I still look at that gold medal every night before I go to bed and think of all it represents in my life and in the life of so many others now.

God is my faithful coach through every jump, training session, trial, and competition not just when I ski, but through every minute of every day. And I am eager to face the challenges of each day "through Christ who strengthens me."

The principles and power of God's incredible work is further detailed in the following letters to two soldiers, who so gallantly served their country in the Middle East during the time I was writing this book. You cannot grasp the full message of this book or the full meaning God has for you in this story without reading these letters. They will help you understand the many facets of God's plan for me and for you and the many ways He can turn our trials into trophies.

LETTER TO THE
SOLDIER OF THE 86TH BATTALION

December 23, 2002

Lt. Col. David Dodd
US Army
Fort Huachuca, AZ

Dear Lt. Col. Dodd:

I am writing in hope that you can help me find a soldier in the 86th Signal Battalion. After I spoke at the Christmas Ball, a soldier approached the head table to talk with me. He shook my hand and thanked me for sharing my testimony. He wanted to know if I had written a book about my story. He said he wanted to make sure he had not missed anything I said and would not forget any part of my message.

I told him I had not written a book, but if I ever did I would give him a copy. After he walked away, I realized I did not know his name. This concerned me greatly because this soldier seemed to have a humble and sincere heart. I see those qualities as two of the most important qualities God uses to work in someone's life.

Since I had never written a book before, I wanted to write to this soldier in as much detail as possible some of what God has taught me about overcoming fear and living a life of victory.

This book is my letter to him. If you can find this soldier and deliver this letter, I would greatly appreciate it. He is the only soldier to ask me if I had written a book, so I hope he won't be hard to find.

Sincerely,
John Kennedy Vaughan

P.S. I remember hearing your talk to your men on, "As iron sharpens iron, so one man sharpens another," Proverbs 27:17. Your words have helped me see the competition starting dock in a new light. Thank you for the insight your words on that principle have added to my life.

Dear Soldier of the 86th Battalion,

I hope Lt. Col. Dodd finds you for me. I believe if anyone can find you, he can. I began writing a letter to you and ended up writing the book your question encouraged me to begin. I pray this message reaches you, and I pray that the truths and events I have recorded will provide encouragement to you and to others struggling to fight all kinds of battles, no matter how large or small.

Again, thank you for the sacrifices you and your family make for our country and for my family and me. All my life I was taught that anything worth having comes with a great price and I need to be willing to pay that price. However, two of the most important things in my life—my spiritual freedom and my physical freedom—have come at the greatest price, and I have not paid for either. My spiritual freedom was paid for by Jesus on the cross, and I thank Him for that every day. My physical freedom was and is still being paid for by the men and women of the United States military. Rarely do I get the chance to thank our military, but I want you to know I am extremely grateful.

You are one among the world's most highly-trained soldiers—physically, technically and academically. My prayer is that in high-pressure situations, you will be able to function with a sound mind and use all your training to the best of your ability, knowing God is with you.

I have learned that when everything is on the line, if I am not careful, fear can rob me of a sound mind and render all my training and preparation useless. All the training in the world will do you no good if you can't function with a sound mind. God does not want us to be moved by what we see or hear, only by His word. I imagine a well-trained soldier fighting with fear is in great danger, but a well-trained soldier fighting with power, love, and a sound mind, and acting on God's word presents a great danger.

God and His word will help you overcome the fear that can rob you of a sound mind, slow your reflexes, dim your senses, cloud your judgment, and try to cancel out the skills you've acquired and all the physical training you have undergone. Thinking and acting on God's word brings you great freedom, peace of mind, boldness, and an ability to act with a sound mind while using all your training and preparation to function to the best of your ability, no matter what the circumstances.

I wanted you to know that Cmd. Sgt. Maj. Clay saw the Shield of Strength necklaces in a Christian bookstore in Ciera Vista. Understanding the power of God's word, Cmd. Sgt. Maj. Clay wanted to get them to you guys before you deployed to the Middle East. That's when I got the letter requesting five hundred Shields of Strength for the 86th Signal Battalion. I overnighted the tags and now hear that they were handed out as you guys boarded planes headed to Afghanistan.

On the back of most Shields of Strength is written a prayer called the Prayer of Salvation.

Prayers don't save anyone or get anyone to heaven, but a sincere decision to receive Jesus as your Lord and Savior will.

Jesus said that anyone who comes to Him, He will not cast out. He said He stands at the door of our hearts, knocking. For anyone who will answer that knock, He will come in to his or her heart. The Bible, in John 3:16 says: "For God so loved the world that He gave his only Son that whosoever believes in Him will not perish but have everlasting life."

Romans 10:9–10 says: "For if you confess with your mouth that Jesus is Lord and believe in your heart that God raised Him from the dead, you will be saved. For it is by believing in your heart that you are made right with God, and it is by confessing with your mouth that you are saved."

The prayer of salvation (on the back of the shields) is a simple prayer but a powerful and eternal decision. It reads: "Dear Lord Jesus, I realize that I am a sinner. I repent for my sins and I receive you as my Lord and Savior." When a man or woman first makes this decision, he or she is then instantly filled with the power to overcome anything if he or she acts on God's word. Best of all, that person has secured his or her place in eternity with Jesus.

The Scripture on the first tags I sent to your battalion was from Joshua 1:9: "I will be strong and courageous. I will not be terrified; or discouraged, for the Lord my God is with me wherever I go." Joshua was a great soldier who overcame great odds, fighting with power, love, and a sound mind while acting on God's word.

Because members of the 86th Signal Battalion shared Shields of Strength with soldiers from other units, we have had calls every week from US military chaplains requesting the necklaces.

Shields of Strength are simply a reminder of God's word. I pray they will serve to teach people the importance of having God's word in their hearts. I also pray that the Shields will help teach people to form the good habit of turning to God's word, with or without a reminder, in times of trial and even when the waters are smooth.

When I give a tag away, I remember that my mind and heart can carry a lot more of God's word than these tags can. Best of all, in times of trouble, God will bring to memory His words we have stowed in our hearts.

I believe that the more of God's word you have in your heart, the more you are prepared to face anything with a sound mind, until finally there is nothing that will rock you. I have seen elderly men who cannot be moved with or without God's word, and they are full of fear. And I have seen old men who are unshakeable because they depend on God's word to keep them strong. Yet, these men are full of love, compassion, and wisdom. They are strong, but not hardened; bold, but not bitter; slow to anger, but quick to show gentleness and compassion. They are a source of God's wisdom and grace to many in times of trouble.

You have a great opportunity to grow in God's word. Your whole life will be blessed because you are challenged to endure all things with power, love, and a sound mind. Through your trials, God will build strong character within you.

I pray we will both become old men who cannot be shaken, yet who are full of God's love and wisdom. When I see the United States armed forces, I see a gentle giant. Our country was built on Christ. The men who founded this country were Christians. We are by far the most powerful country in the world, even though we are among the youngest. We cannot be moved, yet we are full of love and compassion.

I am thankful that God holds us in the shelter of his hand, and I am thankful He caused our paths to cross last year. I am glad you were bold enough to come talk with me and encourage me to write these words.

I guess God had this all planned. I don't consider myself to have any more favor in God's eyes than the next man or woman. Acts 10:34 tells us: "God is no respecter of persons." He loves you as much as me or anyone else. I am thankful He allowed me a trial too big to overcome on my own, a trial that forced me to trust Him completely through it. I am thankful God did not give up on me, and that He sent me a girlfriend (who is now my wife) to bring me closer to the truth that set me free. John 8:36 says: "He who the son sets free is free indeed." I can testify to that!

I pray my story encourages you to find the same freedom, and that in turn, your story encourages someone else to do the same. And if we never meet again on this earth, you can tell me your story as we walk together . . . along the streets of gold.

Sincerely, Your Brother in Christ,
John Kennedy Vaughan

"Be anxious for nothing, but in everything by prayer and supplication, with thanksgiving, let your requests be made known to God; and the peace of God, which surpasses all understanding, will guard your hearts and minds through Christ Jesus."

—Philippians 4:6–7